She Outgrew the Wound

Also by r.h. Sin

Whiskey Words & a Shovel

Whiskey Words & a Shovel II

Whiskey Words & a Shovel III

Rest in the Mourning

A Beautiful Composition of Broken

Algedonic

Planting Gardens in Graves

Planting Gardens in Graves Volume Two

Planting Gardens in Graves Volume Three

She Felt Like Feeling Nothing

Empty Bottles Full of Stories

She Just Wants to Forget

Falling Toward the Moon

We Hope This Reaches You in Time

A Crowded Loneliness

She's Strong, but She's Tired

She Fits Inside These Words

Winter Roses after Fall

Dream, My Child

Anywho, I Love You

I Hope She Finds This

I Hope This Reaches Her in Time Revised Edition

Come Back to Me

This Day Is Dark

Beautiful Sad Eyes, Weary Waiting for Love

Ascending Assertion

A Midnight Moon

Read This If You've Been Ghosted

The Year of Letting Go

New Moons

My Dear Wildflower

Serenity's Song

The Quiet After

She Outgrew the Wound

r.h. Sin

The authorised representative in the EEA is Simon and Schuster Netherlands BV, Herculesplein 96 3584 AA Utrecht, Netherlands. (info@simonandschuster.nl)

Andrews McMeel Publishing
a division of Andrews McMeel Universal
1130 Walnut Street, Kansas City, Missouri 64106
www.andrewsmcmeel.com

26 27 28 29 30 VEP 10 9 8 7 6 5 4 3 2 1

ISBN: 979-8-8816-0846-0

Library of Congress Control Number: 2025946221

Editor: Danys Mares
Art Director: Diane Marsh
Production Editor: Elizabeth A. Garcia
Production Managers: Shona Burns and Chadd Keim

You found this book for a profound reason and, because I know that this is no mistake, I believe that the words here will fill your soul with whatever it is you've been longing for. Maybe you're tired, weary of being strong for everyone but yourself. Tired of giving love like it's endless while being fed crumbs in return. Tired of explaining your worth to people who don't even deserve to witness your essence take shape.

Maybe you're here because you're unraveling or because you are piecing yourself back together for the tenth time in silence. Either way, you're here with me in this moment, eyes moving from left to right, fully focused on what comes next.

This page isn't here to rescue you; these words are not meant to be your savior. You've done enough saving and, with every word here, I hope you are reminded that you have always been capable. You have been both the storm and the shelter. You know where it aches, and you know how to heal.

You don't need closure; you seek the truth. You don't need to be softer; you wish to be heard. And in case no one else has said it: you deserve better than the hands that let you go.

Sit with me here; sit with these words like you would an old friend. Cry if you need to. Observe the scars you thought would end you. Reclaim the version of you that kept fading behind the destruction of your heart.

This is your permission to feel it all and still choose yourself, every single time.

You are not too much; you are just existing
in a language they'll never comprehend.

The wrong love will always feel like an unnecessary war.

Truth be told . . . you didn't lose them; you released yourself.

Healing is in no way linear, but you are still rising, ascending, and becoming your highest self.

Your softness was never the problem. You were just gentle with people who could never align with your heart.

The love you desire and deserve will not require you to shrink.

I need you to understand that their inability
to fully love you is not your burden to carry.

Peace has become the standard, not the exception.

You must remember that you are worthy of a love that doesn't push you into moments of suffering.

You are not broken; you are breaking cycles,
ending things that no longer deserve your
energy and time.

Stop calling survival "love." Love shouldn't feel like holding your breath. It shouldn't be the ache in your chest or the silence in your voice.

Sometimes it feels cold to heal. Sometimes it's not brokenness you feel, it's the release and detachment from things that do not align with you.

You're allowed to want more than they're willing to offer.

Their chaos is not your calling. That noise will never be the symphony you require to lead a soft and harmonious life.

Your heart has outgrown begging for bare minimum.

You don't have to settle just because
you're tired.

A heart like yours deserves a love rooted in deep devotion and safety.

Your healing is holy.

You were never hard to love; they just weren’t soft enough.

Before you continue, I want you to breathe. Be still, if only for a minute. Take a breath. Not the shallow kind. Not the survival kind. The kind that makes your shoulders drop and your chest rise, like you've finally remembered you are allowed to exist without tension.

Here, you don't have to perform your pain. You never need to shrink your strength or justify the ways you have survived in the past.

Right now, in this moment shared with you, I want you to understand that these words are like soft foundations for your body to be at rest, pausing, finding peaceful moments in a chaotic world. These words are meant for those who've been saving themselves quietly, daily, without applause.

For the ones still standing after heartbreak tried to bury them. For all the hearts that are relearning softness after years of having to be sharp to remain safe.

I want you to know that you are not too much. You were just never held right. You're not hard to love; you've just outgrown the people who mistook the depths of your heart for difficulty. Let these words hold the parts of you no one clapped for. Let them speak to the nights when your soul felt restless.

Some endings are a rebirth. You have been transforming the heartache into the origin story of how you healed.

Nurture the version of you that has been choosing peace.

She is no longer available for love that feels depleting.

You never really miss them; you miss the illusion and promise that their potential once defined.

Heartbreak is meant to be a teacher, not your home.

You are not too sensitive; you just feel deeply, and there is nothing wrong with a heart that has the capacity to feel things that others are afraid of.

The things that hurt you then inspired the
boundaries that protect you now.

The right love will never force your soul
into spaces of confusion.

She's not healing to be chosen. She's healing to gain the full benefits of what it means to choose herself. The light, the warmth, the consideration that she once gave to others. Now, expressed inward.

Closure is not a requirement for peace.

You started to let go, not out of spite but
because your spirit was tired of pretending
that you were not worthy of more.

You are not crazy for wanting the level of consistency that doesn't lead to unanswered questions.

She is deserving of a love that doesn’t test her sanity.

Eventually, you begin to understand that some levels of silence aren't weakness; it's wisdom gained from saying too much to the wrong people.

She decided that she would no longer be a landing place for broken promises.

I know they mistreated you in ways that have made you question your worth, but in truth, you are the lesson they'll never forget. The ways in which you taught them what it means to lose the best thing to ever happen to their heart.

The red flags are never a challenge; they are warnings.

There is no emotional warfare when you are in love with someone worthy of your heart.

The chaos no longer excites her. Peace is what she requires.

Healing has never really meant forgetting. It means forgiving yourself for all the moments that made you forget who you always were.

She is not a dumping ground for emotional unavailability.

That’s the thing . . . she was never hard to love; they were always hard to trust.

She began to deny your access to her once she remembered that her heart was sacred ground.

I just need you to remember that you are not
losing people; you are losing illusions.

The loneliness is not punishment—it's preparation for a better life, a brighter love.

This time, you're not waiting; you are aligning.

Love doesn't need to hurt to be real.

The end was just your return to yourself.

The heartbreak is meant to refine you, not define you.

A woman's self-awareness is her power. The more she nurtures this gift, the closer she is to all that aligns with her essence.

Your ability to discern will have people calling you difficult, but only because you are seeing the ill intentions they've been trying to hide.

In truth, they didn't break you, they revealed you. They reminded you of everything you were before they attempted to destroy you.

You have been evolving into the woman
your younger self prayed for.

Never explain your worth; embody who you are, and they will see.

You stopped protecting their potential so that you could protect your peace.

Clarity is a love language.

Detaching from the people who enjoy destroying your nervous system is a form of self-love.

No longer am I available for emotional
chaos and a "love" that feels uncertain.

Love is not something you wrestle with. It is a tangible thing that provides rest.

This era represents the refusal to romanticize red flags.

I hope you know that there is no love in going backward. There is no love in returning to the place where confusion exists.

She's choosing softness with structure.
A sustainable love, rooted in a wild that
feels safe.

Let every "no" remain sacred.

In this era, she refuses to negotiate her boundaries.

This is the era when her heart is no longer impressed with potential.

Healing is necessary, but you don't need to be fully healed to be lovable.

You are allowed to say, “This is not enough;
I need more.”

In this era, she is no longer loving others in hopes of being loved back.

She began to realize that she wasn't waiting for someone, she was just meeting more of herself.

This moment of loneliness is not empty; it's fertile ground where all of what you are has a greater chance to grow and bloom.

I'm proud of you because your self-respect
has outweighed your fear of being alone.

You are no longer in a season of your life
when you believe love is something to
beg for.

She's been learning to be her own peace.

True love should feel like rest, not resistance.

in truth, she didn't rise
because it felt poetic
she rose
because no one was coming
and the silence became dangerous

there were nights
she begged the darkened sky
for softness
only to be met with
more lessons on how to survive

love had left her
with questions
and no one stayed
long enough to answer

but she refused to wait
she started building altars
from the pain
spread out within her heart
lighting candles
for the woman she was becoming

not softer but wiser
still healing while making
a complete commitment to herself

she has become
the quiet aftermath of a storm
that learned how to love itself

healing has never been loud
it's this quiet decision
to refrain from begging
to be chosen by someone
who lacks the capacity for love

loyalty, in its purest form
should never push you
into decisions of self-abandonment

they call a woman cold
because she refuses
to burn to keep them warm

she survived
by no longer explaining
her feelings
to the person
who attempted to destroy her

no mirror
just stillness
the space to remember
the silence to find your voice
the time to cultivate
the courage needed
to let go and move forward

she stopped chasing closure
the moment she realized
her peace was louder
and more profound without it

that version of her
that begged to be understood
no longer speaks

it was tough
but loving herself
meant grieving the parts of her
she gave to people
who never earned them

he failed
he didn't necessarily
break her heart
he exposed the parts of her
that still believed in potential
over proof

she was never hard to love
they were just too lazy
to fully act on the promise
of something life-changing
because they lacked the ability
to do it properly

she outgrew the things
that prefer her broken

in truth, my dear
they never actually loved you
they loved how easily
you believed a lie
that presented itself
as everything you thought you needed

and the moment you woke up to the truth
your heart became a place
they could no longer reach

that version of you
was never bitter
she was just exhausted
from being used
and then blamed
for her sadness

you were certain
and so, when you walk away
you move closer to a truth
that has always existed in your heart
and the more you choose yourself
the more distance you put
between yourself and the people
who had always hoped you'd remain
confused

you stopped explaining yourself
the moment you discovered
that they only heard what they wanted
and ignored your every scream
for all the things you knew you deserved

You never needed saving; you just needed to remember. And somewhere within these pages, I hope you began to fully hear your own voice again. That soft one, the strong one, the one that has often been drowned out by the noise of people who never deserved to speak a word into your life.

This book alone has become a sort of mirror, and now, as you reach this moment, you are seeing more of yourself, truly, fully, without the need to apologize. There's no going back to being misunderstood just to feel less alone . . . taken, but taken for granted.

You know better now, about yourself and the world that surrounds you. Deep down, you know what love is supposed to feel like when it's genuine. You've outgrown the ache that used to define your existence. You have learned that closure can be quiet. That healing isn't perfect, but it can still be entirely yours. And that your story doesn't end here, it begins when you finally choose your whole heart without guilt, hesitation, or permission.

Close the book, not because the story is over but because you have now outwritten everything that ever tried to hold you back and break you.